Hospitality Property Organizational Structure

Hotels-Resorts-Inns-Bed and Breakfasts-Vacation Homes

By

Gerry MacPherson
Keystone Hospitality Property Development

Legal Disclaimer

The information presented here is based on years of experience and does contain some of our own personal feelings and practices. The contents are not the only way to operate a hospitality property but we would highly recommend looking at this information as guidelines and food for thought.

We understand you are serious about the operation of your property, this has been proven by your purchase of this book and asks that you honour our efforts by abiding by our copyright guidelines.

Copyright

http://www.keystonehpd.com

Table of Contents

1. Who We Are

We are Keystone Hospitality Property Development, a group of travel experts that have come together with decades of hospitality property (hotels, resorts, inns and bed and breakfasts) visitation experience.

We have spent 1000s of nights in properties of all sizes and classes worldwide, conducting countless site inspections for many world-class tour and travel companies, as well as received feedback from 100,000's of customers.

This knowledge has given us a unique insight into the wants, needs and requirements of individual and group travellers, management and employees. We understand what it takes to make a hospitality property successful as well as practices that can ensure failure. This book is designed to get you started on the right track and if followed, when you open the doors to your independent hotel, resort, inn or bed & breakfast, you will be on your way to becoming successful.

2. Where To Start

For the sake of this book, I'm going to assume you're either starting from scratch or are hoping to grow your current business.

Let's go through a step-by-step process

2.1 Sleep around
Visit other hospitality properties in the area you're considering opening. Talk with the owners and find out their pros and cons.

2.2 Don't be rushed to find the right location

If you're dealing with a real estate agent, find one that's willing to take the time to find you the best deal. If you feel you're being pressured by them, my first instinct is to always walk away.

2.3 Study the surroundings

I was once chatting with a gentleman who wanted to buy a hospitality property, sitting on a cliff overlooking the Atlantic Ocean. The building was in great shape, beautiful view and loyal clientele and the current owner were selling for a very low price. He wanted to know my opinion, so I asked him what the rate of the cliff erosion was. He had no idea and admitted, he never considered it. Upon further checking, we found that the cliff was eroding at an average of three metres a year and at that rate, he would have to move his property within 10 years. This was a cost he had not considered and passed on the deal. Examples of how elements could affect a site.

- *Is the area prone to flooding?*

- *Where the winds come from?*

- *Other considerations could be is there industry in the area?*

- *Heavy traffic or livestock farms nearby?*

You have to be aware of the noise and potential smell.

Before committing to a site, visit it on several different days and times so you'll understand what your guests will experience.

2.4 Make sure your design fits

Building an independent hotel, resort, inn or bed & breakfast in an industrial zone is probably not the best way to attract your ideal guest.

- *Is there an infrastructure in place?*

- *Do the roads make your property easily accessible?*

- *Is public transportation usable?*

- *Are there things for your guests to do? Restaurants or attractions?*

"Details like this are extremely important"

Alright, you found the right spot. Before you do any building or renovating you have to decide —

- *Who is your target market?*
- *Are they going to be vacationers or business travellers?*
- *Young or old?*
- *Wealthy or budget travellers?*

You should have a target market in mind and not try to be everything to everyone. Now, that you know your target market, you are going to have to determine their needs and this can be done by researching other properties targeting your market, trends and technology.

When designing your hotel, resort, inn or bed & breakfast, it will be well worth your while to hire an architect or designer who understands the hospitality industry. Interview them away from your site, their office and ask to see work they've done. When you feel comfortable with your choice, then bring them to your site.

Use the appropriate consultants as necessary; for example;

- *interior designer*

- *structural*

- *landscapers*

- *electrical*

Etc.

Benefit from their expertise but remember you're in charge. Overseeing this kind of development can be very time-consuming and if you're unable to do it yourself, hire someone you trust to manage the project.

"Create a budget and stick to it"

2.5 Walk and visualize everything

You want to draw out every aspect of your property and even a better option would be to have a three-dimensional model built. You want to understand how all aspects of your property will work together before the first nail is hammered or concrete is poured. I had mentioned you need to have a budget and stick to it but it's also important to be flexible when necessary.

2.6 Set a schedule and an end date

Make sure everyone involved agrees to and signs on to the schedule and completion dates, keeping in mind any outside factors that could influence this time frame. For example: holidays, legal requirements.

Frequently visit the site to make sure there are no surprises and as each operational area is finished, do walk around, looking at it as your guests would. When the building renovations are almost complete and you might be thinking...

"I can hardly wait to open the doors and invite the world in, everything is almost done."

Not so fast!

Your property might almost be ready but now you need an organizational strategy in place. In chapter 8, I am going to be looking at setting up your organizational strategy, but before I do that, I will take a look at the hospitality industry, the history and different types of property's.

3. What Is The Hospitality Industry?

The foremost focus is customer satisfaction and this can play an important role in both leisure and business. A welcoming, substantial reception and entertainment for guests, visitors, or strangers extending not only to hospitality properties but anyone who wishes to provide customer satisfaction.

Without satisfaction, an organization would quickly lose customers. That said, the hospitality property sector is more heavily reliant than any other on customer satisfaction. You have to think of customer satisfaction not being a marketing tool but the main service offered.

4.1 What does hospitality mean for hospitality properties?

For hospitality property owners or staff members, your goal is to ensure your guest's experience at your property is excellent. In a hospitality property setting, your guest exists to be served, you as a provider exists to serve. A provider succeeds when they make a guest feel comfortable and catered to. It's delivering this experience that brings guests back and drives repeat revenue. For your guests, hospitality is the thing that buffers their anxiety, monotony, or fatigue and treats them with enjoyment and relaxation. It gives them an experience that replaces other emotions from the day. They are willing to pay for it and are only satisfied if their expectations are met with the service they receive. For hospitality to be good, as a guest, they have to feel comfortable and well-served.

Think about it this way.

Hospitality is the guest experience, a combination of items offered plus the service quality in which those items are offered. It's not your guest's responsibility to remember your property. It is your responsibility to remember the guest without fault and to deliver service that makes them never forget you.

"What does hospitality mean if the customer has a positive experience?"

That means you've done your job!

4. History Of The Hotel Industry — How We Got Here

You are an aspiring or seasoned owner, manager in the hospitality property industry, hotel, resort, inn, bed and breakfast etc.

How did we get here? Do you know where our industry started?

Hotels or a version of have been around for a couple of thousand years going back to the Greeks and Romans who offered lodgings next to their thermal baths, resort towns and along routes popular with the rich, traders and politicians. They were also found along caravan routes in the Middle East.

In the Middle Ages came the increase in the popularity of the monasteries and abbeys. They offered a bed and a supper to all the travellers, not just the politicians and the rich. They were inns, with small rooms, often for share, taverns, stables and houses of the owners all in one place, and they started to appear all around Europe. There were no amenities but the bed bugs were free.

By the 17th century, the coaching inns became very popular. They offered travellers food, changed their tires and tended to the horses. Around this time wealthy folks began travelling more for fun - but they wanted more for their money. Due to this demand, the hotel industry we know today slowly began to form.

The late 1700s saw the first publicly held hotel, the City Hotel in NYC and in 1829, the first modern hotel, the Tremont House, opened in Boston. This hotel was a site of luxurious firsts: a reception area, free soap, locked guest rooms, bellboys and perhaps most important of all, indoor plumbing.

Later in the 1800s saw the expansion of rail and in Canada the opening of the grand railway hotels which conveyed class and charm.

The hotel industry truly skyrocketed with the launching of passenger airlines.

International and even intercontinental travels were significantly shortened giving travellers more time to explore their destinations and creating income for the hoteliers. As airline competition grew, flights became cheaper and available for a wider audience.

Then came the Internet.

This global system of computer networks changed the world. Hotels could now advertise and gain more visitors. With the emergence of Online Travel Agencies, it became easier for travellers to find the hotel they liked and book without leaving the comfort of their own home. Then they could rate their stay and either persuade travellers to go to a certain location or warn them to stay away.

Now, the traveller's choice of a hospitality property to stay in has increased dramatically. From a huge modern hotel to a designer property, to a bed and breakfast, to an ice hotel, to an Airbnb, to a botel, to a pod and on and on and on.

There are still those who are happy with just a place to sleep but for most travellers, the bar for the hoteliers/innkeepers has been raised very high and it has become increasingly more difficult to please guests. For that reason, it is imperative to continue to learn and *#MakeTheirExperience*.

5. Types of Hotels Throughout the World

"Have you ever noticed there are many different types of hotels throughout the world?"

This chapter will include the property terms from the most common accommodations to the most obscure, with definitions.

1-Star Hotel — A *one-star hotel* is a designation for a hotel that meets minimum standards of service and quality, but offers just the bare essentials as far as amenities, service, and decor. Exact inclusions and exclusions vary depending on the country, government oversight, and star ranking scheme.

2-Star Hotel — A *two-star hotel* is a designation for a hotel property that is usually reasonably priced and offers minimal services, amenities, and decor. A good option for budget travellers that want a bit more than the no-frills scene at a *one-star hotel*. Exact inclusions and exclusions vary depending on the country, government oversight, and star ranking scheme.

3-Star Hotel — A *three-star hotel* is meant to be slightly above average as far as service, options, and amenities. Exact inclusions and exclusions vary depending on the country, government oversight, and star ranking scheme. Modern conveniences and on-site hotel staff can be expected at most 3-star properties.

4-Star Hotel — A *four-star hotel* offers a deluxe level of service, whether for business travellers or those on vacation. Hotel guests can expect luxury amenities, a range of hotel services, and excellent decor. Exact inclusions and exclusions vary depending on the country, government oversight, and star ranking scheme.

5-Star Hotel — A *five-star hotel* is the highest standard in just about every hotel ranking system. Guests at *5-star hotels* and resorts can expect luxurious rooms, attentive staff, unique art, fine dining restaurants, spa services, and more. Exact inclusions and exclusions vary depending on the country, government oversight, and star ranking scheme.

7-Star Hotel — A *seven-star hotel* is a new, unofficial designation for a few high-end hotel properties around the world, mostly in the Middle East and Asia. Started as a marketing scheme, about a dozen hotels now exist which bill themselves as *7-star hotels* and resorts. Features go way above those at "normal" hotels, with some offering a fleet of Rolls-Royce Phantoms, helicopter services, or a 24-carat gold iPad in every room.

Airbnb & Similar Businesses — Although not considered a hotel, is a place where a host has space to share and offers travellers a place to stay for a fee.

Airport Hotel — An *airport hotel* is a property that is situated within an airport's transit zone, on the airport's property, or close to an airport. Known also as *transit hotels* when inside an international airport's transit zone, airport hotels offer connecting travellers the convenience of nearby accommodations. Some may even offer rooms at an hourly rate to give travellers a few hours to change, shower, and nap between flights.

Albergo Diffuso — The *Albergo Diffuso* is an Italian hospitality-concept aimed at reinvigorating small, dying towns by making several distinct places (e.g., town hall, brewery) each into a unique "room" of this dispersed hotel. The *Alberghi Diffusi* (plural) gives guests a unique opportunity to witness the life of the small town from within.

Apartment Hotel — An *apartment hotel* is a hotel property located in an apartment building and offering similar decor, appliances, and amenities as renting an apartment would, but with hotel services such as reception also available. Apartment hotels are also known as serviced apartments or residential hotels and are similar to extended-stay hotels.

Bed and Breakfast — A *bed and breakfast* is a small form of lodging which offers guests a room for the night and a communal breakfast the following morning. Many *bed and breakfasts*, known as a *B&B* or *BnB*, are large family homes minimally converted to allow for guests to rent out bedrooms for their stay. A host or hostess, often the owners, welcomes guests, helps with any needs and provides breakfast in the morning.

Boarding House — A *boarding house* is a larger house, often someone's home, where the owner rents out a room or rooms to guests for one or several nights. Some *boarding house* owners may provide extra services, such as laundry and meals.

Boatel — A *boatel* is a water vessel that has been converted into a hotel for a unique form of accommodation. A *boatel* "room" may be as simple as a fishing boat docked at a pier with a canopy over it and a bed inside, or more extravagant, such as a large riverboat offering dozens of rooms and travelling from place to place, such as a *hotel barge*. *Boatel* may also be spelled as *botel*.

Botel — See *boatel*.

Boutique Hotel — A *boutique hotel* is a small hotel property that distinguishes itself from nearby hotels and worldwide properties by offering guests unique services, features, decor, and more. *Boutique hotels* usually have between 10 and 100 rooms and may host a particular theme, similar to theme restaurants. Themes may revolve around environmentally-conscious services, fitness, or just about anything else.

Bunkhouse — A *bunkhouse* is one of the no-frills types of hotels where workers in small or remote towns may stay for the night when in transit. In the United Kingdom, *bunkhouses* are similar to *hostels*, though offering much less in the way of tourism services.

Capsule Hotel — A *capsule hotel* is a hotel type where small capsules, barely larger than a regular person, are available to host the guest for a quick nap or overnight stay. Since they are so small, *capsule hotels*, also known as *pod hotels*, may be stacked atop one another. Guests may have to climb small ladders over other capsules to reach their own.

Casa Particular — A *casa particular* is a Cuban homestay concept similar to *vacation rentals* crossed with *bed and breakfasts*. A regular homeowner may rent out a room as a *casa particular* and offer breakfast or other meals in addition to the bed.

Casino Hotel — A *casino hotel* is a hotel property with a large casino as the anchor tenant on the ground floor. *Casino hotels* are common in gambling destinations, such as Las Vegas.

Chain Hotel — A *chain hotel* is a hotel that is part of a group or family of similar hotels under a single brand name.

Choultry — A *choultry* is a resting place for travellers, particularly pilgrims to important Buddhist, or Hindu temples in and around Asia.

Coaching Inn — A *coaching inn* is an all-but-defunct type of lodging once popular in Europe for hosting weary travellers between European towns and cities. A *coaching inn* may also be known as a *coaching house* or a *staging inn*.

Condo Hotel — Essentially the same as an *apartment hotel*.

Convention Center Hotel — See *conference hotel.*

Conference Hotel — A *conference hotel*, or *conference centre hotel*, is a hotel that is connected to or part of a conference centre. Visitors to conferences staying at *conference hotels* have the convenience of being the nearest to the scene, and perks are offered in package deals. *Conference centre hotels* may also be called *convention centre hotels*.

Doss House — See *flop house.*

Eco Hotel — An *eco-hotel* is a hotel aiming to make the least environmental impact possible. *Eco hotels* often use sustainable materials, promote environmental consciousness, and aim to reduce and reverse climate change effects.

Extended Stay Hotel — An *extended stay hotel* is a hotel property offering rooms with all the amenities of modern living for guests expecting to stay longer than a typical vacationer. Rooms at *extended-stay hotels* may offer microwaves, ovens, refrigerators, and more closet space to accommodate long-staying travellers.

Flop house — A *flop house* is not a particular hotel type, but rather an old slang term used to refer to the worst types of accommodations. *Flop house* is an American term, and the British equivalent would be a *doss house*.

Garden Hotel — A *garden hotel* is a type of hotel, usually a large residence converted into paid accommodations, notable for its large and detailed outdoor gardens, often created and designed by famous botanists.

Gasthaus — A *Gasthaus* is a German lodging type where a public bar, restaurant, or banquet hall includes accommodations for overnight guests in the back or upstairs.

Green Hotel — See *eco-hotel.*

Guest House — A *guest house* is a type of lodging meant to accommodate an overnight sleeper. It can refer to many things, depending on the context and location, from a smaller house attached to a large estate or one of several places rented out, similar to a *villa.*

Heritage Hotel — A *heritage hotel* is a hotel that often has historic importance, such as converted castles. Many decorate the hotel rooms similar to the era that the hotel originated.

Heuhotel — A *heuhotel,* a German word meaning "hay hotel," is a type of hotel where guests pay to sleep on hay bales or beds formed from hay. Some *heuhotels* have private rooms with beds made of hay, while others are shared rooms, like a hostel. Many hotel proprietors complete the experience by establishing the hotel in a converted barn.

Holiday Cottage — A *holiday cottage,* sometimes known as a *vacation property* or a *holiday home,* is a small house (or sometimes an apartment) used specifically for vacation housing. Usually, the property's owner rents out the *holiday cottage* to guests for a fee (such as on Airbnb), but sometimes the owners use it as their own holiday home, which makes it in this case a second home.

Homestay — A *homestay* is usually a private residence offering accommodations to paying guests. However, when referring to volunteering abroad opportunities or similar situations, *homestays* may refer to the fact that the volunteer will be hosted by a local family for the duration of their volunteer duties, rather than at a central headquarters.

Hostal — A *hostal* is a cheap type of hotel found in Spain and Latin America, offering perhaps a small café or bar and a private room for rent. A *hostal* differs from a *hostel* in that it is usually family-run, similar to a bed and breakfast.

Hostel — A *hostel* is an inexpensive lodge for budget travellers where people from different parties can stay in shared dormitories on bunk beds, usually.

Hotel — A *hotel* is an establishment primarily offering multiple rooms for overnight guests. *Hotels* may include much more than just rooms and reception, such as spa services, restaurants, bars, and more.

Hotelship — A *hotelship* is a large boat, river ferry, or cruise liner which serves as a water-based hotel. While a *boatel* is often meant to hold just one party of guests, a *hotelship* can accommodate dozens or hundreds of passenger guests and may go from one place to another during the stay.

Hotel Barge — A *hotel barge* is a popular type of lodging in Western Europe, mainly France and the United Kingdom. A trend from the 1960s, commercial river barges put out of service were converted into accommodations for travellers seeking a unique form of lodging. The *hotel barge* is often referred to as a *péniche hôtel* in French.

Ice Hotel — An *ice hotel* is a hotel constructed of ice blocks and packed snow, usually a seasonal novelty rather than a year-round place of accommodations. While most of the construction is made of ice and snow, such as the walls, furniture, and bars, some fixtures and parts, such as doors, are of regular, non-ice construction.

Independent Hotel — An *independent hotel* is a hotel not affiliated with any *hotel chain* or other hotel property.

Inn — An *inn* is usually considered to be a rural or suburban lodge accommodating travellers for overnight stays. The *inn* concept may have started as far back as the Roman Empire, where inns were set up along the *via Romana* (the Roman roads along the Roman Way).

Love Hotel — A *love hotel* is a short-stay hotel meant to give guests a private room designed for sexual encounters. Guests at *love hotels* sometimes called *sex hotels* can often book by the hour or by the night.

Luxury Hotel — A *luxury hotel* is a hotel that aims to offer guests a luxurious lodging experience. *Luxury hotels* are usually 4-star and 5-star hotels (and those 7-star hotels).

Microstay — A *microstay* is not a type of hotel (though there are some *microstay hotels*), but rather it is a booking type where a guest stays less than 24 hours, usually in 3-hour increments. Some guests book a *microstay* for long layovers to just get a brief nap, while others use it for trysts, but these are usually at *love hotels* specifically made to accommodate short sexual encounters.

Motel — A *motel*, short for "motor hotel," is a hotel designed primarily for travellers by car. *Motels* often offer doors directly on the parking lot, for easy access to personal vehicles.

Patient Hotel — A *patient hotel* is a hotel specifically designed to accommodate medical patients who need to be near a hospital but don't necessarily need to have a hospital room. A *patient hotel* is also great for housing friends and relatives of a hospital patient. These are common in the Scandinavian countries.

Péniche Hôtel — See *hotel barge*.

Pension — A *pension* is a smaller hotel, akin to a *guest house* or *bed and breakfast*, usually offering guests three full meals per day. Common in Europe, northern Africa, and in the Middle East, *pensions* are usually small affairs run by the owner. They are usually cheaper than branded hotels, but they also offer far fewer amenities and services.

Pension Hotel —A *pension hotel* is a Philippines-specific *pension* offering bare-bones living arrangements, but at prices much lower than regular hotels. Rooms in a *pension hotel* are often empty except for a bed, air conditioner or fan, and maybe a chair.

Pod Hotel — See *capsule hotel.*

Pop-Up Hotel — A *pop-up hotel* is a temporary hotel, often set up to take advantage of seasonal events, marketing opportunities, or other fleeting moments. *Pop-up hotels* may set up in one place, get broken down, and re-establish themselves in another location immediately after, or they may be a one-time thing.

Railway Hotel — A *railway hotel* is a hotel built inside or next to a train station, similar to an *airport hotel.*

Residential Hotel — See *apartment hotel.*

Resort — A *resort hotel* is a hotel that provides many vacation-related activities, amenities, and services, more than a standard hotel would. *Resorts* may include multiple swimming pools, a variety of bars and restaurants, services such as kayak rentals, and child-minding areas.

Roadhouse — A *roadhouse,* also known as a *stopping house,* is similar to a rest stop along a highway which provides some entertainment, a bar, and meals. Back in the day, *roadhouses* often also offered guest rooms, but most now do not. A *roadhouse* with lodging was comparable to a *coaching inn.*

Ryokan — A *ryokan* is a type of inn in Japan that features traditional Japanese furnishings and layouts. You can expect to find tatami mats on the floors, yukata-dressed guests, and communal baths.

Serviced Apartment — See *apartment hotel.*

Sex Hotel — See *love hotel.*

Ski Resort — A *ski resort* is a *resort hotel* built on or near a large skiing park or mountain, established primarily for guests looking to ski or snowboard rather than regular tourists.

Staging Inn — See *coaching inn.*

Stopping House — See *roadhouse.*

Suite Hotel — A *suite hotel* is a hotel offering only suite-level accommodations, such as *junior suites, mini-suites, master suites*, etc. They do not offer regular hotel rooms.

Timeshare — A *timeshare* is a type of property ownership scheme where multiple people buy a property and own specific weeks of the year, allowing them to visit that property or rent it out to others when their week comes each year.

Transit Hotel — See *airport hotel.*

Turbaza — A *turbaza* is a type of Soviet-era lodging, usually consist, include or compose a large building located in a getaway location, such as a forest or secluded beach. *Turbazas* often have dozens of rooms, so large groups, such as family reunions or company outings, would rent it out entirely for their group. *Turbazas* are common still in Ukraine, Russia, and several other eastern European countries.

Vacation Home — See *holiday cottage*.

Vacation Rental — A vacation rental is a place that is rented out to someone for an overnight stay. Vacation rentals are often rented out by property owners and maybe a single room or the entire property. Vacation rentals are often listed on Airbnb or other similar websites.

It might be worth your while to go through the list again and pinpoint exactly what you offer. It could help with your branding and marketing.

6. Hospitality Property Departments & Definitions

I am going to list the departments you would find in the average branded hotel. In a smaller or independent hotel, resort, inn or even bed and breakfast you will find the same departments but the chances are that individual employees, managers and even owners could find themselves taking on more than one role.

6.1 Front office department

The front office department is considered as the nerve centre of a property. These are the employees that often are the only ones with direct contact with guests, other than in the restaurant staff. Front-office employees welcome & register guests, give them their room keys, carry their luggage, and answer questions about the events & attractions in and around the property, then check them out. Also included in their responsibilities are taking reservations, working reception, assigning rooms, and the settlement of guest bills.

6.2 Housekeeping department

The housekeeping department is responsible for the cleanliness, maintenance, and visual upkeep of rooms, public areas, back areas, and surroundings of a property and the pristine upkeep of all guest rooms and public spaces. To be successful in the housekeeping departments employees need an eye for detail and a commitment to the training, development and to be motivated. It is the service and cleanliness of a property that really can have an impact on guests and can be a determining factor in whether they will return or recommend a property to others.

6.3 Food and beverage service department

This department looks after the service of food and drinks to guests. Culinary preparation, as an art and science in the modern kitchen, required more than just a knowledge of food being prepared and the methods of preparation. It is through a knowledge of basic skills, terminology, and rules of the kitchen that a final goal, preparation and service of quality is achieved.

6.4 Engineering and maintenance department

The engineering and maintenance department looks after the maintenance of all the equipment, furniture and fixtures at a property. They are also responsible for repairing and maintaining the external and common area lighting, water treatment and distribution, boilers and water heating, sewage treatment, plant and machinery, fountains and water features etc.

6.5 Accounts and credits department

This department maintains all the financial transactions. Such tasks can include invoicing customers, accounts receivable monitoring and collections, account reconciliation, payables processing, consolidation of multiple entities under common ownership, budgeting, periodic financial reporting as well as financial analysis. Also, common are setting up adequate internal controls for handling external audits and dealing with banks to obtain financing.

6.6 Purchase department

The purchase department is responsible for attaining the inventories of all the departments of a property.

6.7 Security department

The security department of a hospitality property is responsible for the overall security of the building, in-house guests, visitors, day users, and employees and their belongings.

6.8 Human resource department

The H. R. department is responsible for the acquisition, utilization, training, and development of a property's human resources. It is also responsible for the administration of an impartial and internal justice system that will promote transparency and openness in organizational communication.

6.9 Sales and marketing department

The major role of the sales and marketing department is to bring in business, increase the sales of a property's products and services.

6.10 Information technology (IT) / systems

The Information Technology department is responsible for the day-to-day support of all IT systems, business systems, office systems, computer networks, and telephone systems throughout the hospitality property.

7. Setting Up Your Organization

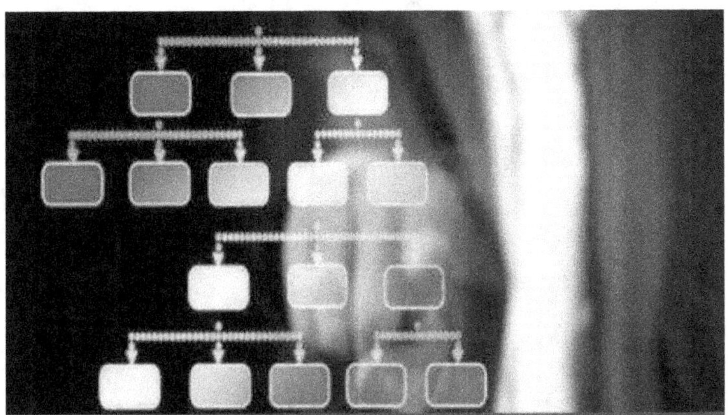

If your goal is to have your hospitality property working for you rather than you working for your property, you must take the time to set up your organization.

7.1 Your organizational strategy

This next section is about setting up your organizational strategy but before we do that there are a few other things that have to be determined.

Why are you or wish to be a hospitality property owner?

What made you decide you wanted to run an independent hotel, resort, inn or bed & breakfast?

7.1.1 Do you fall into one of the following categories?

- *You realized at an early age this is what you wanted to do. You went to school specifically to learn how to operate a hospitality property.*

- *You grew up as part of a family-run operation and you operate your property the way you've seen them operate in the past.*

- *You bought into a business opportunity because it looked interesting or exciting and felt this is something you wanted to try.*

- *You worked hard or most of your life in an industry other than hospitality and were looking for a change, a new lifestyle.*

Do any of these sound familiar? I'm interested in your story, so if you would like to share feel free to contact us via, Twitter, Facebook, LinkedIn or even email. The reason I asked why you would like to become a hospitality property owner, hotel, resort, inn or bed & breakfast, is that this helps determine where you see yourself in the operation of the facility.

7.1.2 What type of owner are you

Are you a business opportunist?

- *Someone who has created and owned their own businesses in the past and is always looking for a new experience.*

- *Someone who sees an opportunity in many things and knows they can turn it into an exceptional business.*
- *Someone who loves using their imagination, always looking forward, never living in the past*
- *Someone who loves to dream and create.*

Are you a supervisor?

- *Someone who thrives on order*
- *Someone whose mantra is "If it's not broke don't fix it"*
- *Someone who can foresee problems*
- *Does not like change*

Or are you a skilled worker?

- *This skilled worker is the doer; do it yourself if you want it done right.*
- *The skilled worker who is in today.*
- *Multitasking is not in a skilled worker's vocabulary, you do one thing at a time and do it right*
- *You feel if you don't do it, it doesn't get done or it doesn't get done right.*

Can you see yourself in any of these categories?

Which of these categories is more valuable when operating an independent hotel, resort, inn or bed & breakfast?

"Can you see any problems trying to be all three?"

The business opportunist is always looking at new great ideas, dreaming of how things can be.

The supervisor wants everything done in an orderly fashion, to stay within the system and the budget.

The skilled worker knows what has to be done, and does not like the idea of their routine is disturbed.

Today's typical small business owner is only 10 percent business opportunist, 20 percent supervisor, and 70 percent skilled worker; and in most cases, this is out of necessity.

Do you think a better balance would be more advantageous for your business?
If you don't have balance, there are going to be parts of your business that are lacking.

What steps do you need to take to become a more balanced operator?

7.1.3 What are your Main Goals?

You should get used to the idea that your business will have an important role in your life, your business isn't your life. Therefore, to begin developing a balanced business, you have to answer these questions:

- *What do you personally value most in life?*
- *What kind of life do you want to lead?*
- *What do you want your life to look like when completed?*

- *Who do you wish to be -- deep down?*

Most great business people, in fact, great people, in general, can see the way they want their lives to develop. Until you can answer these questions and explain to them you cannot develop your business properly.   The biggest difference between successful and less successful people is that successful people don't wait for things to happen. They work on their lives ... they don't exist in their lives. Consider the way you look at things, the way you ask yourself or others questions, the way you focus on situations around you. For example, instead of saying *"Why are bad things always happening to me?"* ask yourself and focus on *"How can I turn this situation around quickly and effectively and feel good about it at the same time?"*

Instead of repeating to yourself *"Why am I such a loser?"* Ask yourself *"How can I become an incredible, motivating, hospitality property owner who LOVES this amazing life?"*

You might be thinking, sure changing questions, but that's not going to help me change the way I feel inside. OK, you're right, you're going to have to start working on how you feel inside and you can do this by trying the following exercise:

- *Write down 20 things you love about yourself*
- *20 things you're grateful for*

Keep the list nearby and refer to it whenever things get tough. You should also keep answers to your main goals with the two lists.

Doing these exercises and referring to them every day will help you keep your focus.

Be accountable!

As U.S. President Harry S. Truman said *"The buck stops here."*

A central belief of most personal development philosophies is that to have a wonderful life one must take complete responsibility for it and everything that happens. As the owner of an independent hotel, resort, inn or bed & breakfasts, you and you alone have manifested any problems or uncomfortable situations that have occurred. Passing blame to or not being supportive of your employees, can develop a disease that can destroy your business and have a negative influence on your life.

Your problems don't go away until you take responsibility for them.

Alright you might be thinking *"This stuff is a little heavy, I just want to know how to set up an organizational strategy."*

The reason for these exercises is that so when you have an organizational strategy in place and have it work, you have to have the right mindset. You have to be able to look at the big picture. Your goal, in setting up an organizational strategy is to develop a business that you could someday sell or turnover to someone and the operation would continue to operate without missing a beat. You want to develop an operations manual.

You don't have to sell but with this thought process in mind, it will be easier to stay focused. Now, I understand every hospitality property, independent hotel, resort, inn or bed and breakfast could be a little different but this is a model that if you follow, will work. Don't plan on racing through this exercise, it's going to take time.

I recommend that you take some quiet time, away from all the action, a pen and notebook, and write down all the responsibilities required to run your property. When you feel this is complete, assigned headings to the responsibilities. I don't mean individual names but instead titles. When doing this exercise you have to think of yourself as a corporation, not an owner of a business -*Remember, the big picture.*

7.1.4 How you start

What job functions would you need in your corporation?
You need a:

President or CEO (chief executive officer):
This person is where the buck stops. This person is responsible for the overall achievement of the property; all the managers' answer this person and this person is responsible to the investors or shareholders.

Operations Manager:
This person is responsible for keeping guests by providing to them what is promised by the marketing department, and for discovering new ways to make the operation more efficient and to provide clients with better service.

Marketing Manager:
You don't have a business if you don't have people staying with you. The marketing manager is responsible for finding new

guests and retaining old guests. This is done by finding and promoting new ways to target the preferred customer and then providing these customers with an excellent experience at a competitive cost.

Human Resources Manager:

This person is responsible for recruiting and hiring the appropriate people with the appropriate positions. But it doesn't stop there. They maximize employee performance by ensuring each employee is properly trained and fully aware of the employer's strategic objectives; development of performance appraisal, and rewarding (e.g., managing pay and benefits); the balancing of organizational practices with any governmental laws.

Finance Manager:

This person is responsible for both the marketing and operations departments' budgets, ensuring the property is profitable and by securing funds when needed but the best rates available.

Salesperson:

Depending on the size of your operation, this is a person whose sole responsibility is in the marketing department or could be part of the responsibility of other employees. For example, front desk or reservations.

This is the same as an *Advertising or Research* person. Full-time position or an additional responsibility in another position. *Housekeeping Manager, Front Desk Manager, Maintenance Manager, Restaurant Manager,* and on and on.

If you have a small operation, this might sound insane but in many cases, one or more of these responsibilities could fall to one person. The important thing to remember is that each of these responsibilities has to be treated like a separate entity and by this I mean each of these responsibilities has to have its easy-to-follow duties, methods to do each duty effectively, and checklists to ensure they are done correctly.

As I mentioned earlier the president is responsible to the investors and shareholders. When looking at the big picture, you have to see the investors or shareholders as outside the day-to-day operation. Their main concern is that they are making a profit.

For those of you who are planning to or are operating an independent property on your own, you might be wondering who the shareholders might be. You are.

So, now that you decided which departments are necessary to run your operation and assigned the appropriate names *(you might see your name there quite often)*.

Now take the time, and I can't stress this enough, take the time to determine all the duties that fall under each department and how they are done. When I say how they get done, look at the most effective way and what tools are necessary to complete each task. Document this in the simplest form, and I don't need to sound disparaging here but it should be written so that a child could understand.

Talk to your colleagues, brainstorm, and come up with easy-to-understand methods to complete each task that will, in turn, save you time and money. When this is done for every duty that is necessary to operate your property, you will have an operation manual that can be used for training and guidelines for you and your employees.

Once the operation manual is completed to your satisfaction and agreed upon with your staff you will see a vast improvement in the consistency of your operations, which will ensure better customer service, employee happiness and increased profits.

Sample of an organizational structure.

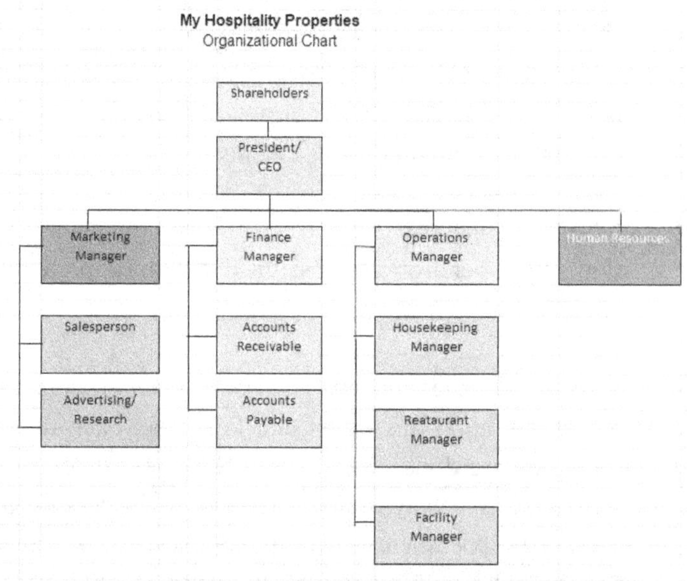

Housekeeping Manager, Front Desk Manager, Maintenance Manager, Restaurant Manager, and on and on.

8. Your Management Strategy

Now, I am going to be taking a closer look at your operations manual.

In the last section, we looked at who you were and what job descriptions were needed to operate your hospitality property. We also talked about assigning the right people for each job, determine the specific tasks for each job and what is required to complete each task. This was to be done in an easy-to-follow, step-by-step checklist form. When all the checklists are completed and compiled you have a working *operations manual.*

I would now like to dive into the actual operations manual itself, what is it going to look like, and how is going to be used.

When opening up your completed operations manual, you should have nothing but a series of checklists and the checklists should be easy to find. To do this you divide your checklists into categories and each category is assigned a colour. For example,

- *Housekeeping-blue*
- *Customer service-red*
- *Breakfasts-green*
- *Accounting-yellow*
- *Maintenance- orange*
- *And on, and on, you get the idea.*

Each checklist details the specific steps each housekeeper, front-desk agent, maintenance person, accountant etc, must take to do their job. The checklists have to be very specific, with step-by-step instructions of what to do and in what order.

8.1 Let's take a look at housekeeping

When a housekeeper opens a door, they do not always know what they will find. The last guest might have been extremely tidy and the room looks as good as it did when the guest first arrived or the room could be turned upside down. My main instinct with the first room would be to start with the bathroom. My instinct with the second room would be to grumble and then start with the bedclothes.

What's the difference between these two scenarios?

I wasn't consistent and when you're not consistent, you miss things.

Today, when I open a room door, I would have a checklist in my hand and regardless of what the room looked like, I would start on my immediate left. I would check the closet to make sure the guest did not forget anything; I would check the lamp to make sure the lights so worked and were plugged in. I would look in the dresser drawers to make sure the extra pillows and blankets were there. I would continue around the room checking off my list as I went to make sure nothing was missed.

My checklist would have a drawing of that particular room on the back of the page and as well as checking off my list, I would check off each area on the drawing as my tasks were completed. I would do the same in the bathroom, kitchenette, at the windows, and under the bed. My checklist would also have a space for any repairs required and if necessary, I would fill out a request for maintenance form. The checklist would cover every detail of that room and when the checklist and drawings were all marked finished, I would feel confident that this room was complete. I would then sign the bottom of the checklist confirming everything is done.

Now, you might have some employees who do not like the idea of being monitored like this. I've heard some say they felt like children. Have you ever gone to the grocery store knowing you had to pick up three items, get to the store and only remember two of the items?
If you had a checklist, this would not be a problem.

If you run into this problem with employees not wanting to change, ask them how they would feel the next time they took on a flight, they found out the pilot and co-pilot did not do a preflight check or the next time their car was in for a safety inspection and the mechanic just looked at it and said *"looks good to me"*, without looking under the hood or when their child was in to see the doctor and the doctor just touched their head and said *"perfectly healthy"* ... they might be a little concerned.

We have all heard the stories of the person going in for an operation and having the wrong leg amputated or lung removed. This happened because doctors went into the operating room assuming they knew what they're doing. More and more hospitals are incorporating checklists into their day-to-day procedure.

You might say, these are very important, of course, they should do more checking. Well, your business is very important and employees with a good work ethic are very important for your business. With this step-by-step system in place, you will be ensured your employees will retain consistency and the chance to show real pride in their work.

Okay, back to housekeeping.

So, the housekeeper arrives in the morning and checks their mailbox (they should have a mailbox) to find which rooms will be vacated that day and to get the appropriate package of checklists to go with each room. These would be prepared the night before by you or your night auditor. Each room package would include the room checklist, maintenance or repair requests, and any special requests for incoming guests, as well as any other checklists you feel necessary.

As each room is completed, both the front and back of the checklists are signed, and then this package goes to their immediate supervisor. The supervisor can then do follow-up or spot checks to make sure nothing was missed. This should not be taken personally, as in even the most organized companies there are times when things are missed. If this does happen regularly however, there might be grounds for reassignment or dismissal of the employee.

With a system like this in place, even a brand-new employee would not require weeks or even days of training and monitoring, instead, they would be turning over rooms like a pro in no time.

Let's look at customer service as another example.

You have a returning guest, and that guest has a file that indicates they had taken advantage of your spa during their last visit. When the customer arrives, your front-desk agent follows a checklist that includes, check guest's likes and dislikes, they know to ask *"Would you like me to book your spa appointment for this afternoon or tomorrow?"* This is before the guest has even mentioned the possibility of a spa appointment.

They might not have planned to use the facility, but now given the option might consider taking advantage. This is an excellent example of how a checklist could work for an upsell. We'll talk more about upselling later in the book.

So, you might ask, *"What else should I have a checklist for?"* the simple answer-

EVERYTHING!

- *When the outdoor lights turn on*

- *How much fruit should be in the bowl at reception and what it should look like?*

- *What bills have to be paid and when*

- *What items are recycled?*

- *How the towels should be folded*

- *How a uniform should be worn*

You get the idea, everything should have a checklist, with diagrams.

If you have this system in place and work it properly, there will rarely be any errors — it works! In no time, you will be amazed by the number of people to come up to you and thank you for the way they've been treated. In many cases, this will be due to the consistency which happens because of your checklists.

You might be thinking, *"Following the same checklists every day, is going to get boring for me and my employees?"*

I should mention here that if your operation manual is complete and used properly, it's worth its weight in gold but that does not mean it's set in stone. It has to be treated like a living, breathing entity.

If your employees are working off their checklists and come to you because there are aspects of it they do not like, you ask them *"Okay, how would you change it?"* and if they come up with a way that will improve the service and or save your business money, change it! And after you change it, reward your employee. This can be done financially, with gift certificates or time off, if possible.

The only guideline you should have is that *"Any criticism is constructive and with an alternative option."*

I have seen when employees have been given this type of freedom in the development of their work routine, they have come up with some great ideas and in turn a wonderful sense of pride. I am interested in hearing from you.

Do you have a system in place that works?

Do you use hard copy (paper) for your system?

Or are you more high-tech, using tablets or computers that link directly to a database?

On the following pages, I have included sample checklists for room inspection, maintenance requests and a lost and found form. Please feel free to take them and use them as you see fit.

Guest Room Cleaning Checklist

This is a very long list but you can customize it to your property and your particular rooms
We would like to know what items we might have missed

Items	Yes	No
Door lock works properly		
Door opens easily & quietly		
Light switches work properly		
Windows open & close properly		
Window glass clean		
Window glass free of cracks		
Drapes straight & working properly		
Controls for air conditioning/heat work properly		
Air conditioning filters clean		
Lamps work		
Wall lights work		
Lamp shades clean & straight		
Beds correctly made		
Bedspreads straight		
Fluffed/Even pillows		
Rate cards posted		
Is the mattress firm		
When was the mattress last turned		
Bedspreads free of rips & stains		
Upholstery clean & in good condition		
Furniture scratched or stained		
Walls clean & free of cobwebs		
Walls scratched or nicked		
Luggage racks in good condition		
Pictures and mirrors straight		
Furniture drawers slide easily		
Telephone working		
Clean ashtrays & matches		
Mattress pads clean & free of stains		
Light bulbs with proper wattage		
Minimum of 6 hangers (3 suit, 3 dress)		
Drapes partially closed		
Desk tops		
Dresser Tops		
Table Tops		
Headboards		
Chairs		
Picture Frames		
Mirrors		

Rim of baseboard
All drawers
Closet shelves
Closet rods
Telephone
Lamps & shades
Light bulbs
Window cornice
Window frame
Corners
Window sills

The Bathroom
Clean toilet seat (both sides)
Underside of lavatory clean
Shower rod in good condition
Commode clean under rim
Commode flushes properly
Bathroom free of odours
Shower curtain clean
Pop up stopper clean
Water spots on tile
Tub grouting missing
Tub grouting clean
Supply of towels
Faucets leaking
Broken Tile
Toilet seat firm
Fixtures firm
Chrome sparkling

Credenza
1 Guest Directory
1 Hotel Evaluation
1 Laundry bag & laundry slip

Night Table/Desk
1 Bible (night table)
1 Pocket Folder w 3 envelopes/3 stationery
1 clock radio
Internet connection
WiFi

Closet

3 hangers + 3 hangers w skirt clips

General

1 ice bucket & poly liner
1 waste basket
3 ashtrays in guest room (smoking only)
1 memo pad with pen
3 wrapped glasses
1 telephone book

Bathroom

1 display tray
2 bars Brand facial soap, 1.25 oz
1 bottle Brand shampoo, 22ml
3 bath towels (four in double, doubles)
3 hand towels (four in double, doubles)
3 face cloths (four in double, doubles)
1 bath mat
Hairdryer

Miscellaneous

1 coffee maker
1 filter pack of coffee or
1 filter pack of decaffeinated
1 tea bags
1 condiment package
1 Iron
1 Ironing Board
1 refrigerator
2 coffee cups, porcelain

Guest Room Settings

Room:

Lights	Off
Heating	Set at 18ºC or 70ºF
Windows	Closed
Drapes	Closed
Television	Off

Bathroom

Sink Faucet	Off
Drain Plugs	Open
Shower Curtain	Centered Inside Tub
Shower Head	Point Towards Wall
Toilet Seat Lid	Down
Bathroom Door	Open
Tub Faucet	Off
Light	Off

My Independent Hotel or
Bed & Breakfast Name & Logo

<table>
<tr><td colspan="4" align="center">MAINTENANCE REQUEST FORM</td></tr>
<tr><td>DATE</td><td></td><td>TIME</td><td></td></tr>
<tr><td>ROOM NO</td><td colspan="3"></td></tr>
<tr><td>LOCATION</td><td colspan="3"></td></tr>
<tr><td>REPORTED BY</td><td colspan="3"></td></tr>
<tr><td colspan="4">PROBLEM</td></tr>
<tr><td colspan="4" height="200"></td></tr>
<tr><td>ASSIGNED TO</td><td colspan="3"></td></tr>
<tr><td>DATE COMPLETED</td><td></td><td>TIME SPENT</td><td></td></tr>
<tr><td>COMPLETED BY</td><td colspan="3"></td></tr>
<tr><td colspan="4">REMARKS</td></tr>
<tr><td colspan="4" height="200"></td></tr>
<tr><td colspan="2" align="center">SHIFT IN- CHARGE</td><td colspan="2" align="center">SIGN</td></tr>
<tr><td colspan="2" height="150"></td><td colspan="2"></td></tr>
</table>

LOST & FOUND – Enquiry Response Letter

Dear (Salutation + Guest name),

Regretfully the item mentioned on your correspondence email / mail mentioned as being lost, has not been turned into our Lost and Found Department.

I have personally checked our Lost and Found log and the security locker.

(In case additional information is required about the lost item)

I have enclosed a request for additional information form and please provide the details.

The information you have given me now will be kept on our file. If your missing item should be turned in future, then we will inform you accordingly and also we will make necessary arrangement to courier you the same at the following address:
Mailing Address as per the hotel records:

____
____
____

Regretfully,
(Hotel Name)

Name
Executive Housekeeper

Annexure - Lost Item Inquiry form

First Name: _____________ Last Name: _______________

Room No : _____________ Check -out: _______________

Email : _____________ Mobile No : _______________

Item Lost: _____________ Lost Where: _______________

Additional Description:____
____
____
____

9. What Should Your Operation Manual Include

In the last section, I looked at the frame or the structure of the operations manual as well as a couple of examples of what it should include. Next, I'll be looking at specifically what should be in an operations manual. I'm not going to tell you exactly what your operations manual should include because it's up to you. The material could vary a little bit from property to property but the frame or structure I'm going to share with you is universal. I do suggest keeping a pen and paper handy in case you think of additional information you would like included.

Okay, here we go

It should include the following:
- *Company History, Vision & Organization*
- *Products & Services*

- *Policies*
- *Position Statements*
- *Systems (how it's done)*

Statistically, nine out of every 10 businesses fail within the first five years, this is why you should not look at your hospitality property as an independent business.

If you look at McDonald's, Starbucks, big chain hospitality properties, more of them succeed because they are set up for consistency — they are franchises and 75% or more of franchises succeed. Part of the reason for their success is due to having a standard operation manual in place. If you're a small property, your chances of success will increase dramatically if you are determined and take the time to develop an operations manual.

As I mentioned before, your operations manual should be treated as a living, breathing entity and can be amended accordingly as trial and error findings are made.

When designing your manual, you must always have in the back of your mind,

"Can I open a second location with this operations manual model and not have any problems?"

or

"Can I open 10 locations with this operations manual model and not have any problems?"

or

"Can I open 1000 locations with this operations manual model and not have any problems?"

Your goal must be to develop the best working system of the operations manual model and when it's complete your system must work like clockwork.

"What should go in your operations manual model?"

As I said before

EVERYTHING!

An example I have used in the past is McDonald's.

The next time you walk into one of their locations, take a moment to look at their operation.

2. *Look at the décor of the restaurant*
3. *How you are greeted by the employee*
4. *Their uniforms*
5. *The distance between the ovens-to the burger slides-to the register*
6. *How the fries are cooked on a timer*

In theory, no matter what location you find yourself in a McDonald's restaurant all the above will be the same. The reason, they are all working from the same operations manual model. You may or may not enjoy the franchise but there is no way you cannot respect their system.

You might be thinking...

"I'm in the small hospitality property industry, why are you talking about McDonald's?"

That is easy, the theory is the same. It's an operations manual model that works so, there is no reason for you to try and rediscover the wheel, copy a model that works and use it. Your operations manual will contain a large amount of information including, a detailed organizational role responsibility list *(who was responsible for what, with a diagram if applicable)*

9.1 What else to include in your operations manual model?

The location of your site
   Description:
7. *The amount of foot traffic you attract*
8. *The amount of drive-by traffic you attract*
9. *Area and your customers' demographics (age, sex, lifestyle)*
10. *Distance from a population centre*
11. *What is your highway access like?*
12. *The distance to complementary businesses.*

Reason:
   Your location will tell you a lot about your business. Is your location easily accessible to your target clientele?

Training
   You must have this aspect of your operations manual model correct. The training must be step-by-step, and easy to understand by even the lowest possible skill level. You should also be specific on how your training will proceed.

When the employees are hired or change positions?

Not so preferable

Regularly?

Preferable

Who is responsible for the training and what are the necessary materials needed?

Your Properties Set-up

What equipment, furnishings, and accessories are required? Include prices if possible.

Supplies and Inventory

This would include: room supplies, bedding, towels, bathroom accessories, cleaning supplies, vacuum cleaners, marketing materials, if you have a restaurant food inventory etc. You'll also include the quantity, the supplier or suppliers, the price etc.

Your Staff's Uniforms

You have to decide how you would like to present to you and your staff to your customers. Professionally dressed or casual? Is the dress consistent and does it have your business name and logo?

Marketing Efforts

What is the marketing you use? Who is your target customer? What are the platforms and the percentage of your marketing budget allocated to each?

Personnel

a. Responsibilities

An organization chart of the duties and who is responsible. Including whom is responsible at every level is very important in this section. Also, include who is to follow-up.

b. Perfect employee profiles

What skills are necessary for each role? The type of personality required? Do they have to be team-oriented?

c. Job descriptions

Refer to the organizational chart and be more specific.

d. How do you find your potential employees?

Where do you recruit, how do you recruit, would you call for referrals?

e. Interviewing and background checks

A prepared list of interview questions for each position. How to do background and referral checks?

f. Pre-employment testing

The policy and procedure for pre-employment testing.

g. New employee orientation and training

A new employee orientation and training process. This must be thorough and consistent.

h. Communicating and personnel policies

Having a proper communication system in place is crucial to the success of your operation.

i. Paying your employees

When and the system to be used, as well as the procedure for bonuses.

j. Scheduling for employees

How are vacations handled, time off requests, and a plan to make sure all is fair and consistent.

k. Employee management forms

This is for current and new staff to review old and new procedures. Ongoing training.

l. Employee morale / motivation

Would you like to come to work every day to the same old day and day out routine, nothing ever changes? Neither would your employees. It is important to keep your employees motivated and to have systems in place to accomplish this.

   a) *Keep track of what factors create good morale*
   b) *Signs of bad morale*
   c) *Ways to improve motivation and morale*

m. Performance evaluation

When and what is the standard? Are they once a year, twice a year or ongoing? What is the system you use? Do you have a motivation component included in your evaluations?

n. Employee discipline

Here it is extremely important to document everything.

o. Documentation – witnesses - signatures.

i. *Resignation*

ii. *Termination*

iii. *Post-separation procedures*

iv. *Final paychecks*

v. *Explaining termination to other employees*

vi. *Giving references*

p. Good employee management practices

What practices and gratitude policy do you have in place for employees and management?

10.2 Daily operating procedures

What is your hospitality properties operating procedures

When will you be open?

Customer Service Procedures

Here you cannot have too much detail. Great customer service is the lifeblood of your business.

a. *Customer service viewpoint*

i. *Customer feedback*
   How you will judge the effectiveness of your system?

ii. *Customer complaints*
   A customer complained process

iii. *What is your customer complaint policy?*
   This has to be step-by-step.

iv. *Refund requests (Your policy?)*

b. *Service procedures*

This is done to consistently provide great customer service. For example.

    v.   *Greeting customers*
    vi.   *Answering the telephone*
    vii.   *Atmosphere*
    viii. *Understanding the product offerings*
    ix.   *Working / interacting with customers*
    x.   *Job descriptions*
    xi.   *Suggested selling techniques*
    xii.   *Passive selling versus active selling*

c. *Do you have merchandise?*

Does your merchandise fit with your business's image?

    i.   *How will it be displayed?*
    ii.   *Will there be signage?*

d. *Meal preparation procedures*

Here again, consistency is very important.

    i.   *Prepping procedures*
    ii.   *Setting up the stations*
    iii. *Consistent recipes*
    iv.   *Preparation procedures for everything*
    v.   *Maintaining inventory*
    vi.   *Dishwashing / Sanitation procedures*

e. *Transacting sales*

You don't want your employees figuring this out on the fly as they are ringing up a customer, so they have to know:

    i.   *Cash handling procedures*
    ii.   *Accepting personal checks*

iii.   *Accepting credit cards, debit cards*
iv.   *Suggested prices*

f. Gift certificates
    i The Issuing of gift certificates
    ii Redeeming gift certificates

g. Inventory management
    i   What is the minimum inventory level before ordering?
    ii Who orders?
    iii How much is ordered?
    iv Who is the supplier?
    v   What is the price?
    vi What are the order procedures?
    vii How to change suppliers
    viii Receiving procedures
    ix Storing procedures
    x   Labelling and inventorying rotation
    xi What to do with spoilage
    xii How is waste handled?

h. Operational and financial reporting

You might be surprised to hear that I have met many hospitality property owners and managers that are so nervous about their books that they ignore them. Keeping weekly profit and loss income statements have to be at the top of your list as well as tracking the metrics of your business.

    i Who is responsible?
    ii What and when reports should be generated
    iii Analyzing the reports

i. *Loss prevention techniques*

How are you going to audit for theft? What is the policy for documenting and follow through on suspected theft?

    i   Cash
    ii Inventory

j. *Required cleaning and maintenance*

Dirt in the corners or cobwebs on the ceiling is a major turn-off for me. It has been my experience that customers tend not to return to dirty establishments, especially if you handle food.

So what is your ...

    i   Daily cleaning and maintenance
    ii Weekly cleaning and maintenance
    iii Monthly cleaning and maintenance

k. *Safety procedures*

Employee time off due to a preventable accident or injury can be very difficult for employee morale and your bottom line. Safety programs can go a long way, an ounce of prevention is worth a pound of cure.

    i   Preventing accidents and injuries
    Ii Crisis management policy
    iii Reporting accidents
    iv Worker's compensation issues
    v   Fire safety
    vi Robbery / Burglary
    vii Unruly customers
    viii Using the alarm system

l. *Sales procedures*

How are customers handled from the initial contact i.e. reservations, to after they arrive home?

    i   Introduction

    ii The sales process

        a)Identifying the customer's needs

        b)Building rapport

        c)Handling objections

    iii Understanding your competition

    iv Competitive advantages

    v   What is your sustainable advantage over your competitors?

    vi What do you consistently do well?

This can be shared with pride.

m. *Marketing*

    i.   *Promoting your business in your area*

    ii.   *Logo specifications (your brand is your business's soul).*

    iii. *Required marketing budget*

    iv. *What platforms will you use for marketing*

How will you get the message out and what methods will you use to gauge the effectiveness of your campaigns? What is your message?

- *Direct Mail*
- *Radio*
- *Television*
- *Billboards*
- *Magazines*
- *Newspapers*

- *Social media*
- *Networking*
- *Word of Mouth / Customer Referrals*

n. Community involvement

Some of the most successful businesses are those that give back. Your top-line goal should be to serve as many people as possible. Your profit will follow.

i. *Press releases*
ii. *Better business bureau /or similar associations*
iii. *Local Chamber of Commerce / or similar associations*
iv. *Team sponsorships*
v. *Community service / charitable activities*

o. Management documents

This is an incredibly important aspect of your business – it allows your managers to have a consistent execution of the policy you have instilled and it provides consistent tools across the board.

i. *Daily cash sheet*
ii. *Absence policy*
iii. *Applicant information release*
iv. *Sample applicant rejection letter*
v. *Sample applicant acknowledgment letter*
vi. *Time spent during work hours*
vii. *Customer satisfaction survey*
viii. *Discipline documentation form*
ix. *Drug Test consent form (if applicable)*
x. *Electronic funds transfer authorization*

The now after seeing all of this, some of you might be thinking

"Wow, Gerry you're killing me, I only have a small operation."
The let me remind you of the statistics I shared earlier.

"9 out of 10 businesses fail within the first five years. 75% percent of businesses using an operations manual model succeed."

Now, the reasons could include many factors such as your name, your marketing success and people skills to name a few but the core of your business will always lie within the operating procedure.

10. How Will I Know My Operations Manual Works?

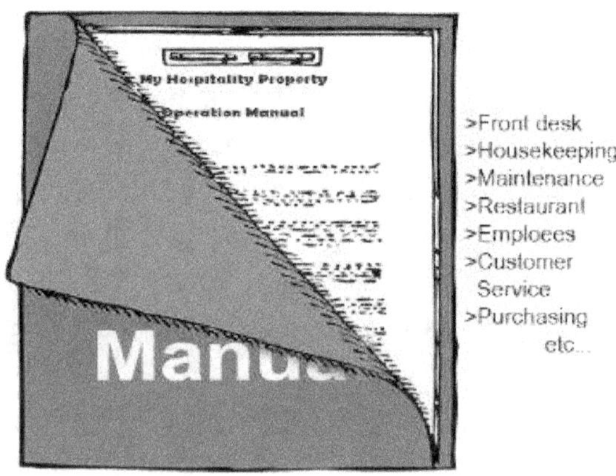

In the last couple of sections, we have looked at your operations manual. We were looking at the framework or the structure, and in the last chapter, I gave you examples of the type of forms you would want to include. I understand, to some of you, the list might have seemed extreme, but I am serious when I say, you have to have documentation for everything.

Okay, you've got your organizational structure in place, everybody knows their responsibilities, their duties and how to perform them step-by-step.

Now, you have to ask yourself *"When it is complete, will it work?"* To know this you have to ask yourself another question, *"Will the concept, my operations manual be saleable?"* And then you have to ask *"Will I be able to clone it? And if so will it provide good returns?"*

Yes, I want you to look at your business as a product and this is a product you want to sell.

No, I'm not telling you-you have to go out and sell your property, but for you to know for sure that your operational procedure, your operations manual works, you have to put your head in a different mindset and look at your property as a product. I want to force you to think that the business system you are creating is a business you're going to sell, and it would work once it was sold no matter who bought it and used it as is.

I've had many hospitality property owners tell me they have no idea how they would do this.

It could be difficult for some, and it may sound a little strange for a hospitality property owner that they have to start thinking of their property as a systems-dependent business, not a people-dependent business. Your system, your operations, has to work flawlessly, even without you.

And yes, I've heard.

"Work without me, I'm the heart and soul of this business, it can't work without me."

Yes, I've heard that more than once.

I know it's tough, but thinking like this will not work if you are trying to determine whether your system works. Don't think of yourself as a boss of a hospitality property, but more like an engineer working on a pre-production prototype of a product you want to mass-produce.

You want to think of Henry Ford when he was developing his system to mass-produce automobiles, an assembly line system, and a system that could be replicated over and over again.

Okay, you have to focus, you have to think like Henry Ford and Ray Kroc of McDonald's. You have to think of your hospitality property as a sample, a model of 10, 100's, of 1000s of hospitality properties to come.

At your business, your model will become a place where all your theories are put to test to see how well they work before becoming part of your operations manual and operational in your business. Every possible detail of your business system will be first tested and scrutinized intensively at your property model.

"There will be no detail too trivial, you will have to pay attention to all the little things."

And then what you should soon begin to realize, is that you are now working on your business and not in it.

When you reach that point, you will begin to realize that the purpose of your life is not to serve your business, but instead, purpose of your business is to serve your life.

"Your life and business are two separate things."

You will very quickly begin asking yourself questions differently, instead of saying *"This is a crazy mess, how am I going to fix it."*

You will say *"Our policy for this situation is — this. Is there any way this policy can be improved and if approved, will it work in all situations?"*

You will now be wondering if this clone can be replicated perfectly.

"You are now working the business, business is not working you."

What considerations will you have to take and a factor when working with your property model?

Your property model has to work with people at the lowest possible skill level.

- *Your property model will stand out as a place of incredible order.*

- *Your property model will have a uniform colour (branding), dress and facility code.*

- *Your property model will provide consistent predictable service to your customers.*

- *All the work at your property model will be documented in the operations manual.*

- *Your property model will deliver consistent value to your customers, employees, suppliers and lenders, above and beyond their expectations.*

Now don't get stressed, this is going to be a continuous work in progress with each aspect of your property model going through a natural progression.

- *They will be to innovate the initial thoughts*
- *Measuring the viability and then*
- *Adapting and adding it to the operations manual*

Now you have to set your criteria, your benchmarks.
When do you wish your property model to be completed?
In one year?
Three?
10 years?

Who is your clientele?
Local?
Regional?
International?

Are your clientele
Business people?
Families?
Singles?
What are your criteria regarding customer service?
Food Service?
Cleanliness?
Employee training?
And on and on.

If you don't have firm criteria, your standards will be all over the place.

This is going to be a lot of work, but you don't have to do it all at once, it will be ongoing. To help you through this initial process, I want you to use your imagination.

Imagine, if you will, your property model is working like a charm. Your operations manual has every plausible situation covered. You come to your business every day and it is full of happy customers and fulfilled employees.

A gentleman walks through the door with a sack full of money, and he tells you he has heard all about your business and would like to have one just like it.

And you say to him, *"Let me show you how it works"*.

You guide him through your hospitality property, showing him how each element of your business works and how it works with every other element.

You introduce him to your employees and when he's asking them all kinds of questions, you feel confident and can stand back as they proudly explain how everything works.

You feel comfortable with the thought, you can spend as much time with this buyer as you would like, knowing your business will not be affected.

Imagine, how impressed the potential buyer will be when he sees the cleanliness, order and control.

Imagine how would you feel when he says *"Your property looks good now, but what happens if you have to leave?"* and you tell him *"I'm leaving for a month-long cruise next week, and I don't have a worry in the world"*.

This might sound a little far-fetched but I've seen it work over and over and over again.

There is no question in my mind this could be your life, but you have to start by starting. Start with your criteria, put your organizational structure in place, and determine the tasks that fall under each department along with step-by-step procedures to complete them.

That is how you start.

Slowly, begin developing your property model and build your operations manual.

Will the property model work? *"Yes!"* It does work if worked properly.

It can't be done half-heartedly, it has to be done intelligently, reasonably, intentionally, systematically, and compassionately. If it is worked in the right spirit, it will work every time it's applied because it requires the full engagement of the people working it.

You will notice, that when you constructively introduce the development of your property model, it will create instant positive change in you and the people around you.

"That is the key to its success."

It is important to remember that everybody involved in this process knows the aim and the final goal. When this is done it becomes real and something tangible.

"Is your head ready to explode or is some of this starting to make sense?"

I encourage you to take the time to read the chapters again, have your pen and paper and write down any notes or thoughts you may have.

11. What Is Outsourcing?

In this section, we are looking at outsourcing by asking and answer the following questions:

- *What is outsourcing?*
- *Why would I need to outsource?*
- *When to outsource?*
- *What duties could I outsource?*
- *Where do I look to find outsourcing?*

Alright, there is a bit to cover so let's get started.

11.1 What is outsourcing?

This is a very simple answer, outsourcing is contracting work outside your place of business. This could be down the street to the local accounting firm or off-shore to hire a VA *(virtual assistant — could be a jack of all trades or detailed to a specific task).*

11.2 Why would I need to outsource?

Earlier in the book, I talked about the type of operator you might be; a business opportunist, the supervisor, or a skilled worker. I also said in a perfect world, a balance of all three would be the best. That's not being realistic and I know how difficult that can be. Setting up a great organizational system will help alleviate many responsibilities that are currently falling on your shoulders, but you will find some duties or responsibilities that would be difficult to complete by you or your present staff due to lack of time or expertise.

"This is where outsourcing can help"

Big businesses have long seen outsourcing as a strategy, and today's technology has made it a more accessible tool for small businesses, and for many, outsourcing has made a powerful impact on their growth, productivity and bottom line. Most business owners have great talents, but many times they think they can do it all.

"Does this sound familiar?"

In reality, you might think or wish you could do it all, but if you step back, you will soon realize that there are other people out there that can not only do it better, but also does it cheaper than your time is worth, and the result will be far better. Taking the first steps toward outsourcing can be time-consuming, but figuring out how to build your business with help from outside professionals can offer increased efficiency and profits. By letting go of some of the reins, you will free up more time to focus on more important things in your business.

11.3 When to outsource?

When you and your current employees are unable to manage the day-to-day business of your property, it may be time to consider outsourcing. I would not wait until it was too late. As soon as you see the workload becoming too hectic, but you can't justify hiring new in-house employees, take a look at what duties could be outsourced.

11.4 What duties could I outsource?

These days technology has advanced to the point where professionals can work from anywhere in the world and with little time, you will be able to find extremely qualified professionals. Before you start, just a word of caution, because you can outsource a task doesn't mean you should. Before deciding which tasks you can outsource, take a hard look at your business and determine your strengths and values. There might be some things you like to do or would like to get off your plate, but be careful of the things important to your core business or for security reasons you should not surrender.

Okay, that aside, here are the type of tasks you could outsource.

They fall into three general categories:

Highly skilled, or executives with expertise.

For example, find a human resources expert who could come in a few times each month to provide consulting advice, employee evaluations, motivational programs, etc. This without paying a full-time salary.

Highly tedious tasks

Accounts payable and data entry are a few examples.

Expert knowledge

Examples might include: IT support for your accounting system or your network, social media consultants, web designers. They are all very important tasks, but you or your staff might not have the expertise.

Here are more examples of commonly outsourced duties.

- Virtual assistants
- Marketing directors
- Graphic designers
- Transcriptionists
- Web designers
- HR consultants
- PR directors
- IT specialists
- Customer support
- Accounting
- Tax preparation
- Manufacturing
- Data entry
- Research & Development
- Legal services

- Creative services
- Healthcare services
- Building maintenance
- Supply and inventory
- Purchasing
- Food and cafeteria services
- Security
- Fleet services
- Video creation

and the list goes on

11.5 Where do I look to find outsourcing?

You want to make sure you find the right outsourcing partner. The first place you should look is in your backyard, your neighbourhood. Ask other business owners or your accountant, lawyer, or banker if they can recommend a provider offering the services you need. Using online platforms such as LinkedIn and Twitter makes it easy to expand your networks and are places to ask for recommendations. If that does not work for you, other options could include placing ads on work-at-home websites, for example:

Flexjobs - *http://www.flexjobs.com/telecommute/employers*
The Home Worker - *http://the-homeworker.com*
Upwork - *https://www.upwork.com*
Work at Home Mom Revolution -
http://workathomemomrevolution.com
Rat Race Rebellion - *https://ratracerebellion.com*
Workersonboard - *http://www.workersonboard.com*
All Stay at Home - *http://allstayathome.com*

11.6 What is the next step?

After you've found a provider, your work isn't over yet.

Ask for and check their references and then take the time to create a specific contract that outlines exactly what performance is expected. Explain your expectations and the steps included in the job clearly; never assume that contractors are thinking about what you're thinking. It is very important that the requirements and expectations are laid out in the beginning, and don't assume anything. Be prepared, there will be a learning curve on the team member's side, so initially, plan to spend more time with them and as your team member gets better, you will have the freedom to focus on more important tasks.

Once you have spent time with the new member, and they have proven they can do the job, step back, relinquish control, and allow your new team members to do the job you've hired them to do. If you are going to micromanage your outsourcing, the savings in your time will be gone and the whole point of outsourcing will be lost. While outsourcing has its great advantages for a small company, it can have challenges.

If you choose to work with offshore providers, language barriers and time zones could be an issue. However, focusing on making your own communications clear can help overcome confusion for those who are not native English speakers and time zones create more opportunity than inconvenience. Assign a task at night, and the next morning, wake to find it complete and waiting for you.

The benefits of outsourcing offer business owners great advantages. It allows you to build a team of skilled professionals without adding the expense of full-time employees, and to avoid getting bogged down with tasks that can be completed without your attention. It's an inexpensive alternative and a proven strategy for growing a business without letting it take over your life.

When you outsource, you can focus your time, attention and resources on your company's main abilities and spend your time setting new goals and finding ways to achieve them.

Now you have your organizational structure in place, what's your next step?

You have to find the right employees and once you do, you have to know how to keep them.

Pick up the *"Steps To Hiring Exceptional Hospitality Property Staff"* course book.

What's Next …

Operating a Successful Hospitality Property
Just Got Easier…

You're just a heartbeat away from the crucial training, advice & support you need to plan, create & grow a prosperous and rewarding, hotel, resort, inn, bed and breakfast or vacation rental.

Does any of this sound familiar?

- *You have a great idea for a hospitality property, but don't know where to start and how to turn that into a real plan...*

- *You've spent countless hours working your business but your organizational structure is lacking and you're tired of having to do everything yourself...*

- *Your employees are not living up to your standards and the good ones leave...*

- *Your marketing is not working as it should and you're not reaching your target audience…*

- *You feel you're a step or two behind your competition…*

If any of these things ring true, then you already know what a minefield it can be trying to get quality advice & support.

Introducing the Hospitality Property School Group

We are travel authorities that have spent 1000's nights in properties of all classes worldwide, conducting countless site inspections for several world-class tour companies, as well as received feedback from 100,000's of guests.

This knowledge has given us a unique insight into the wants, needs and requirements of individual and group travellers, as well as management and employees.

We provide strategies for, and aid in the growth and development of hotels, resorts, inns and bed & breakfasts to create their brand and goals; as well as increase their bookings and profit while keeping their integrity.

The Hospitality Property School Group is packed with in-depth, practical training and resources on all aspects of planning, building, running and growing a successful hospitality property.

Here is How You Will Benefit:

Actionable Workbooks

Actionable workshops are a series of short mini-courses that you can study and then utilize the best practices for your business.

Courses

The design of the courses is the result of decades of experience that have given us insight into the wants, needs & requirements of hospitality property guests, management & employees.

Resources/Perks

You have access to the free resources download centre designed to help streamline your organizational structure, grow your bookings & increase your bottom line. As a member, you deserve a break. Keystone HPD has created a number of training tutorials, ebooks, audiobooks & video production opportunities and you can SAVE up to 50%.

Member Properties

What makes your property special? Tell us about your property, your region, your success stories, your great employees, your favourite guests. Every month we'll pick our one to highlight on the group site.

Q & As

Do you have a question? Ask them here and let the experts in our community share their thoughts, tell their stories & best practices. In this section, we'll catalogue the best responses.

Community Voice

Have you had any game-changing ideas? Tell us in the "Community Voice" section and we'll share the ones we like here and in the monthly update.

You'll Also Find Material on The Following Topics:

- Your Guests
- Personal/Employee Development
- Facility
- Marketing
- Hospitality Property Checklists
- Trends
- Technology
- Operations Manual Development
- Interviews
- Webinars
- Ted Talks
- *INN*sider Tips
- Podcasts

The Hospitality Property School Podcasts provide strategies & techniques to aid in the growth & development of hospitality properties while increasing patronage & profit.

Within the group, you'll have the opportunity to ask questions, share best practices, promote your property etc.

Plus, be able to watch the training tutorials, the video podcasts and listen to the interviews when it fits into *your* schedule.

This is your group and we want you to benefit to the fullest.

WHAT MAKES THE HOSPITALITY PROPERTY SCHOOL GROUP SPECIAL?

ACCESS TO EXPERTISE
Tap into our decades of experience in the industry.

..NO B.S. ALLOWED

We're not into overblown hype, marketing tricks or jumping on the latest shiny bandwagon. Just straight-talking, honest, proven and practical advice. No B.S. or tricks!

..OUR FULL COMMITMENT

We eat, sleep and breathe the hospitality property industry. The group is our main focus and we love helping our group members achieve success. It's what we do, and we're not going anywhere!

.

Are you ready to take your property to the next level?

.

Get Instant Access to the Hospitality Property School Group!

https://member.keystonehpd.com

In case you were wondering, we have a

14 Day No Questions Asked Money-Back Guarantee

When you join the Hospitality Property School Group, you are fully protected by our 100% Satisfaction Guarantee. If you don't feel like you've received value and you decide you want to cancel any time within the next 14 days, just let us know and we'll send you a prompt refund. No hassles, headaches or hoops to jump through. We're confident that you'll find the Membership Academy useful, and we won't make you beg or invoke any silly rules or conditions - if you're not satisfied within your first 14 days then we'll refund you without any fuss.

Simply copy & click the link for your payment option to join

https://member.keystonehpd.com

Other Business to Take Care of Before You Open Your Hospitality Property

Your hospitality property is a business, so to make sure all the correct documentation and forms are filled out and filed before you open your doors to guests. Now understanding every region and country is different, with the assistance of your accountant, lawyer, consultant, and/or broker, use the following list to ensure you have the accounts and paperwork you need before opening day (then mark renewal dates on your calendar).

They include:
- Conditional use and sign permits (if required)
- Business license
- Business name and/or DBA registration
- Certificate of occupancy
- Account for transient/lodging taxes
- Sales tax account (seller's permit)
- Federal and State Tax ID
- Business checking credit accounts
- Merchant account (to process credit cards)
- ServSafe food certification (if required)
- Health Department inspection
- Fire Department inspection
- Liquor license, if applicable
- Insurance (business, liability, property, and liquor liability if applicable)
- Property management/reservation and accounting software

It does not matter how organized we are, there are times when something could happen that will catch us off guard and we are not sure who to call.

Record telephone numbers for the following services and keep the list on hand for quick fixes to ensure your guests' comfort, enjoyment, safety and your peace of mind.

- Animal Control
- Appliance repair
- Cable provider
- Carpenter/Contractor
- Electrician
- Heat/AC equipment person
- Hot tub repair
- Internet provider
- Landscapers/tree removal service
- Plumbing & drain cleaning service
- Power Company
- Propane gas supplier
- Phone service provider
- Roofer
- Septic tank info
- Snow removal service (don't laugh at this if you live in a warmer climate. At the time of this writing the Southern US is being hit with major storms)

Some of these contacts may not apply or you have others I have not included but this is a good list to start with and if you do have any others we would sure like to hear them.